Alexander Baillie Biography

Tacoma / Seattle business and community pioneer and "father of golf in the West"

By Alexander Thomas Ripley
Great Grandson of Alexander Baillie

Copyright © 2018 Alexander T. Ripley. All rights reserved

FORWORD

I don't remember my great grandfather as he unfortunately died when I was two, but I definitely heard a lot about him from my mother, Mary Ripley, father Alexander Baillie Ripley, and grandmother Jessie Baillie Ripley. I was named after my father, who was named after his grandfather. I have gone by the nickname of Sandy all my life, a nickname given to me by my great grandfather soon after he saw me for the first time. Sandy is a common nickname for Alexander in Scotland. All of this has led me to have an interest in knowing more about my great grandfather. Unfortunately I didn't write down what I heard or ask a lot more questions of my grandmother and father while they were alive so what I remember is a little sketchy. But through a lot of research and help from many I have been able to put together this brief biography of Alexander Baillie. I particularly want to thank the following for their input: Jay Baker, John Baker, Martin Baker, Sam Baker, Constance Johnson, Dex Johnson, Holly Ripley, Mary Ripley, William Ripley, The Tacoma Public Library, and The Seattle Public Library. Also, I give a special thank-you to the Tacoma Historical Society for their support and guidance.

A lot of the history of my great grandfather is tied into the history of Tacoma. If in reading this you are interested in reading more about the early boom days of Tacoma and the challenges of the 1890s depression, there is a wonderful book called "Green Timber". It was written by Thomas Ripley, who is my great uncle and from whom I get my middle name. Thomas' style is entertaining with subtle humor throughout.

Alex at his Palm Springs house circa 1945

Alex's Early Years in Scotland (1859-1880)

- **1859** – Darwin publishes the "Origin of the Species"
  - Victoria was the Queen of the United Kingdom of Great Britain and Ireland.
  - James Buchanan was President of the United States.
- **1860** – First British Golf Open
- **1861** – US Civil War declared and Lincoln becomes President
- **1863** – Lincoln delivers Gettysburg Address
- **1865** – Lincoln shot at Ford's Theater
- **1866** - US Civil War formally ended
- **1869** – Suez Canal opens
- **1872** – Yellowstone becomes first National Park
- **1876** – Alexander Graham Bell patents telephone and first call is made
- **1877** – Thomas Edison makes first recording of human voice
- **1880** – Salvation Army formed

ALEXANDER SMITH BAILLIE (I will refer to him as Alex in this biography) was born September 9, 1859. He was born in Farnell, Scotland, south of Brechin, which is located in eastern Scotland north of Dundee and west of Montrose (see map on following page). It is believed he was born at home.

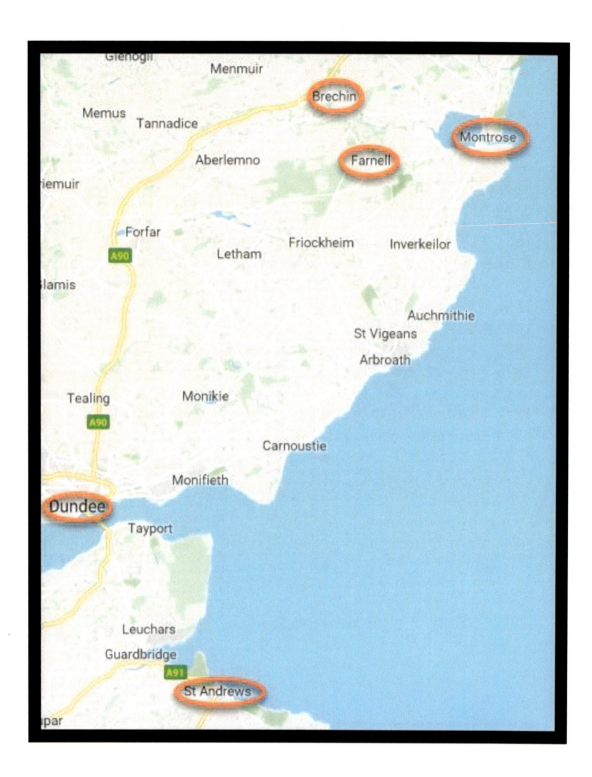

Alex was one of eight children of Alexander (1831 – 1898) and Martha Lindsay Baillie (1832 – 1919). They were married on June 30, 1854. Other children were Jane Ann (1855 – 1859), Martha (1857 -?), Elizabeth (1862 – 1865), David (1864 -?), James (1866 - ?), Susan (1868 - 1947), and John (1870 - ?). Alexander was the keeper of the west gate, where they lived, at Kinnaird Castle near Farnell (see map on previous page) and by trade was a stone mason. His wife was the daughter of the keeper of the east gate.

The West gate keeper's home at Kinnaird Castle.

Alexander, Martha and seven of their children. Alex and his sister Martha are at the top.

Alexander, Martha, with five of their children. Alex is in front of his dad on left and clearly enjoying having his picture taken.

Alexander and Martha are buried at Farnell, Angus, Scotland in the church cemetery.

Farnell church and cemetery

The gravestone for Alexander, Martha, and two of their daughters who died at a very young age reads as follows:

IN
AFFECTIONATE REMEMBRANCE
OF
ALEXANDER BAILLIE
WHO DIED AT WEST GATE, KINNAIRD
29TH DAY OF JUNE, 1898
AGE 66
ALSO OF HIS DAUGHTERS
JANE ANN
WHO DIED AT BRECHIN
ON JANUARY 16, 1859 AGED 4 YEARS
ELIZABETH
WHO DIED JULY 9, 1865 AGED 3 ½ YEARS
BOTH INTERRED
IN CATHEDRAL CHURCH YARD, BRECHIN
ALSO OF HIS WIFE
MARTHA LINDSAY
WHO DIED AT EASTBANK, BRECHIN
15TH DAY OF JANUARY, 1919
AGED 87 YEARS

The Brechin Cathedral above has a three-panel stained glass window given by Alex in memory of his parents. The stained glass was not completed until 1952, three years after Alex died.

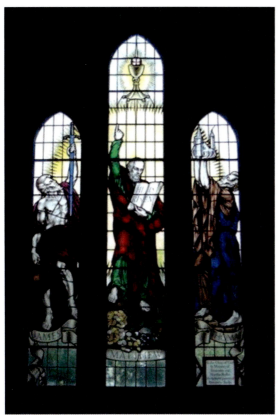
Stained glass at Brechin Cathedral depicting the disciples James, Matthew, and Thomas

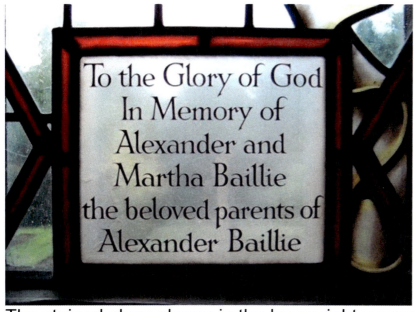
The stained glass plaque in the lower right corner

*****

The Baillies did not have a clan of their own, but Alex was connected by marriage through Martha Lindsay to the Lindsay clan. A connection like this was known as a "sept". Alex's kilt was always of the Lindsay tartan, and he had the full highland dress that he wore for special occasions. Along with the kilt is the plaid (shawl worn over the shoulder with pin), bonnet, doublet (jacket), sporran (purse), dirk (long knife) and sgian-dubh (Scottish Gaelic for short dagger). The kilt and accessories are typically passed to the eldest son. Since Alex didn't have any sons it passed to the oldest grandson who was Alexander Ripley, and when he died it was passed to his oldest son, William Ripley, who will pass it on to his son, Shawn Ripley.

Alex in full Highland dress. Note dagger, known as sgian-dubh (Scottish Gaelic), in sock

Alexander Baillie Ripley in full Highland dress with picture of Alex

William Ripley in Lindsay tartan kilt including plaid, doublet and sporran.

Shawn Ripley in Lindsay tartan kilt and holding the dirk

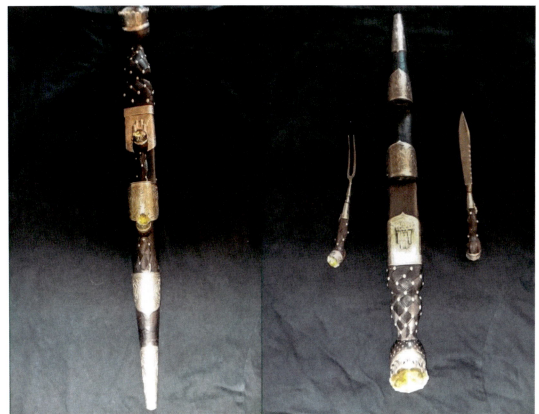

The dirk showing knife and fork that fit in sheath. The stones at the head of the knife, fork and dirk are believed to be topaz.

*****

Alex attended public and high schools in Brechin, from which he graduated at the age of 15. As a youth he was a collector of bird's eggs. He said he fell out of a surprising number of trees and off several cliffs before he abandoned the hobby. After high school he served an apprenticeship in the Royal Bank of Scotland at Brechin, serving the first three years without salary. He eventually was advanced to the position of bookkeeper and then on to assistant cashier but at the end of 5 years he resigned. On October 1, 1879, he went to Liverpool, where he joined the merchant and shipping company of Balfour Williamson & Company. He held a clerical position there for less than a year and before being transferred to Portland, Oregon.

Alex on right as a young man before leaving Scotland

Alex Comes to Portland and Establishes Early Friendships 1880-1885

- **1880** – Thomas Edison establishes the Edison Illuminating Company in New York City. This was the pioneer company of the electrical power industry.
    - Rutherford B. Hayes was the President of the United States
    - 64 inches of snow fell in Seattle over 8 days
- **1883** – Transcontinental Northern Pacific Railroad completed to Tacoma
- **1884** – The Tacoma Hotel opens, "Grandest hotel north of San Francisco" (burned down in 1935).
- **1885** - Mark Twain publishes the "Adventures of Huckleberry Finn"

Robert Balfour and Alexander Guthrie had been sent by the Balfour Williamson Company to San Francisco in 1869 to open a new "House," which was to be known as Balfour Guthrie & Company. It took them 42 days to get from Liverpool to San Francisco as at the time there was no train route across the U.S. They had to sail down the East Coast, then portage across the Isthmus of Panama, and finally sail up the West Coast. They were both in their mid-twenties at the time. In the beginning the two men took the time to explore this new frontier, getting to know the people and potential customers around California. They were quickly successful and by 1873 were making a profit of $100,000 which brought high praise from the headquarters in Liverpool. In the early 1870s they started looking for opportunities in the Northwest. Eventually the Portland office was opened in 1878 by Walter Burns, who had been sent up from San Francisco. It was two years later, in 1880, that Alex was sent to Portland from Liverpool. He was 21 years old. After a few days in San Francisco getting to know the people at the main office he moved on to the Portland office where he became a clerk working for Walter Burns.

Alex was anxious to become involved in his new community and soon sought out the other Scots already living in the area. He joined Portland's St. Andrew Society, which was an organization aimed at providing its members and Scottish immigrant families with material aid such as medical and legal assistance. It was also a networking and social club for the city's Scots where they could celebrate Scottish holidays and festivals. The society was founded in 1875 and as of this writing is still active. Minutes of the society's meetings between 1875 and 1882 were lost in a fire, but minutes from 1883 to 1889 show Alex was elected on November 28, 1884, to a one-year term as one of three members of the Relief Committee. The Relief Committee was the governing body that gave help to the Scottish immigrants as needed. The friendships he made while in Portland would be the basis for their developing the game of golf in the US that they remembered so fondly from their homeland.

Two key friendships that Alex made while in Portland were with Walter Honeyman and Robert Livingston. Livingston was also from Brechin so it is likely that he already knew Alex before coming to Portland. These early friendships formed in Portland would be lifelong, and they often would get together to socialize with some fine scotch or a game of golf. Through the years all three of these friends served as officers in the St. Andrew Society.

During the early 1880s these Scottish friends would sometimes make it out to the Oregon coast. The northern coast of Oregon around Gearhart reminded the Scottish friends of the shores of Scotland that they loved and missed. With both Baillie and Livingston being from Brechin near Scotland's central East Coast they were familiar with golf due to the proximity to the coastal city of Montrose. Montrose is where the famous and historic golf course, the Royal Montrose golf club, was established in 1810. Montrose is only about 42 miles from the legendary and famous St. Andrews course, which had been there since the 15th century. The proximity of Brechin to both Montrose and St. Andrews surely played a key part in both Baillie's and Livingston's interest in establishing golf in the Northwest.

In 1888 Alex was transferred to Tacoma to open a new branch office for Balfour Guthrie Company. But Honeyman and Livingston continued coming to Gearhart and in 1891 laid out the original links course in the sand dunes. Livingston and Honeyman were some of the first people to have vacation homes on the coast at Gearhart. Gearhart was a growing resort town in the 1890s. The Astoria and South Coast Railway completed its tracks between Astoria and Seaside in 1890. The Victorian-style Gearhart hotel was up and running by 1895, and people from all over the region would come to Gearhart to enjoy the beautiful Oregon coast. Golf was seldom heard of at this time in the western United States. The sight of these Scots playing golf on the dunes attracted attention, leaving people to wonder what they were doing hitting a small ball with a stick. Eventually some of the adventurous visitors would join in an informal game of golf and interest in the game grew. This course at Gearhart is believed to be the oldest public course in the country west of the Mississippi.

Alex gets married and starts a family 1885-1894

- ❖ **1886** – Statue of Liberty is dedicated
  - Telephone service reaches Seattle
- ❖ **1888** – Stampede Pass tunnel completed providing the Northern Pacific a direct route to Tacoma
- ❖ **1889** – Washington Territory becomes a state
  - June 6th, Great Seattle Fire
  - Eiffel Tower completed
- ❖ **1890** – The first transcontinental train arrives in Seattle
  - The Tacoma Opera House opened with the largest stage west of the Mississippi
- ❖ **1891** – Carnegie Hall opens with Tchaikovsky as guest conductor
- ❖ **1893** – New Zealand becomes the first country to grant all women the right to vote
  - Financial panic hits the United States on "Black Friday", June 24th

While in Portland, Alex had stayed in contact with Jessie Nicoll (1861 – 1926), a girlfriend from Brechin. He eventually asked her to come to Portland and marry him, which she did. Jessie traveled by ship from England to New York and then on by train to Portland.

They married on May 27, 1885, shortly after her arrival in Portland.

"Mr. Alexander Baillie, chief clerk with Balfour, Guthrie & Co., was married last evening to Miss Jessie Nicoll of Brechin, Scotland, by Rev. Geo. W. Foote, rector of Trinity church, at the residence of Mr. W. J. Burns. The wedding was a quiet affair, only a few intimate friends of the parties being present. Miss Nicoll has just arrived from Scotland, Mr. Baillie having left here several days since to meet her on the way and escort her to the city. The groom is well known here, and is a general favorite with all with whom he comes in contact. The British ships Janet McNeil and San Luis, which are being loaded by Balfour, Guthrie & Co. and the Haideo were gaily decorated yesterday in honor of Mr. Baillie

and the winsome lassie who came so far to make him happy. Captain Jones, of the Janet McNeil, had the motto "Happiness to Baillie – Nicoll" hung between the fore and main topmasts of his ship, in letters of evergreen. Mr. Baillie and his bride will at once commence housekeeping at the corner of Twenty-first and K streets." Oregonian May 28, 1885

Alex and Jessie Nicoll on their wedding day.

Jessie had a brother, George B Nicoll. George came to the Northwest in 1893 from Scotland. George was the first mayor of the incorporated town of West Seattle. While living in West Seattle George was the manager of the West Seattle grain elevator and later became the manager of the United Warehouse Company, a post which he held until 1930. It was in that year that George suffered a stroke which partially paralyzed him. He died in 1936. Jessie also had a sister, Mrs. James Alexander, of Vancouver, British Columbia.

Alex and Jessie had 5 daughters: Jessie (1886 – 1984); Agnes "Polly" (1888 – 1974); Elizabeth (1890 - 1971); Kathleen "Sukey" (1894-1949); and Marian (1897-1947).

Jessie Baillie was born in Portland in 1886. She married William (Billy) Reynolds Ripley (1887 – 1935) on September 15, 1909 in Tacoma. They had one son, Alexander Baillie Ripley. She died in 1984 in Seattle at the age of 98 and is buried at the Tacoma Cemetery next to her husband.

Jessie Baillie Ripley

Agnes "Polly" Lindsay Baillie was born September 18, 1888, in Tacoma. She died in October 1974 at the age of 86, and I believe she is buried in Connecticut. She was engaged to Charles H. Banks in 1913 and they married the next year. They had one child, Janet. They lived most of their lives in either New York or Lakeville, Connecticut. Charles was born June 3, 1883 in Amenia, New York. He attended Yale. Charles died in 1931 at the age of 48 and is buried in Salisbury, Connecticut.

Elizabeth was born in Tacoma in 1890. She married Samuel Lyon Russell September 27, 1911, and they had a son, Montgomery Russell and daughter, Mary Elizabeth (Libby) Russell. Elizabeth and Samuel lived in Seattle. It is believed that she was the first woman to climb Mount Baker. While hiking at Mount Baker she met some climbers who were going to summit and joined them to go to the top.

Elizabeth as a young woman.

She died in 1971 in Seattle and is buried at Lakeview Cemetery.

Kathleen (Sukey) Baillie was born in Tacoma on February 23rd 1894.

Mrs. Alexander Baillie gave a children's party Wednesday in honor of her daughter Kathleen. Fourteen little people were present and were entertained during the afternoon by the older sisters of the little hostess.- Seattle Times February 23, 1902.

Her first marriage was to Capt. William Barrett in 1912. Over the objection of her parents they had eloped. They lived mostly in Portland close to Capt. Barrett's parents, who lived in Hillsboro. They had one son William, and in 1917 they divorced. Kathleen and her son then lived with her parents in Seattle. She then married Commander Isaac Cureton Johnson, USN on May 8, 1920, at Alex's home. They had been engaged for two months. Commander Johnson adopted William.

Masses of Japanese cherry blossoms, with hydrangeas, roses, tulips and sweet peas against a green background gave a beautiful effect to the rooms. The bride wore an exquisite gown of pale blue chiffon with touches of deeper blue and carried a shower bouquet of white orchids and lilies of the valley – Seattle Times May 9, 1920

She eventually divorced Commander Johnson and later married Mr. Ward Winchell. She died December 15, 1949, in Los Angeles, CA, at the age of 55. She is buried at the Tacoma Cemetery near her mother and father.

Marian Baillie was born November 21, 1896, in Tacoma. She married Lieutenant Walter McEwan Tomkins in Seattle on June 15, 1918.

Quite the most startling and sudden marriage of the season was that which was hastily arranged and solemnized yesterday afternoon when Miss Marian Baillie daughter of Mr. and Mrs. Alexander Baillie became the bride of Lieut. Walter McEwan Tomkins USA of Camp Lewis. Orders for Lieut. McEwan to change station were responsible for the hurried arrangements. Bishop Frederick W. Keator read the service at 4:30 o'clock at the home of the bride's parents 907 14th Ave. N. in the presence of the family of the bride and relatives of the groom. The rooms were decked with a profusion of flowers and the bride was charming in a dainty afternoon gown of apricot chiffon. She carried a shower bouquet of white orchids, gardenias, and roses. Plans as to where the bride and groom will be at home are uncertain. Mrs. Thompkins expects to spend much of the time during her husband's expected absence with her parents in the city. She is a charming girl, unusually pretty, vivacious and popular. She is a graduate of Mount Vernon seminary in Washington DC. – Seattle Times June 17, 1918.

She was probably the better athlete of the five sisters being very proficient at both golf and tennis.

At some point she divorced Tompkins. She married Norman A. Goater on January 28 1931 in Seattle. Mr. Goater was from Southampton, England, and had lived in Vancouver, BC. He was the Chief Officer of the Thorpeness which was sunk in 1938 during the Spanish War, but he survived. They had divorced in December of 1937

She died March 22, 1947, in New York at the age of 51. She is buried at the Tacoma Cemetery near her mother and father.

Where the Forsythe name, shown on her gravestone, came from is unclear. At her first marriage in 1918 the Seattle Times listed her name as Marian Forsythe Baillie.

It is believed that Agnes and Kathleen got their nicknames as children from the old English (early 1800s) nursery rhyme with the following verses:

> Polly put the kettle on,
> Polly put the kettle on,
> Polly put the kettle on,
> We'll all have tea.
> Sukey take it off again,
> Sukey take it off again,
> Sukey take it off again,
> They've all gone away.

Alex with four of the five daughters. Left to right are Agnes, Marian, Elizabeth, in front and Jessie.

Jessie with the 5 daughters left to right Jessie (standing), Marian (on her mother's lap), Elizabeth, Agnes and Kathleen (in front).

Jessie Nicoll Baillie on her wedding day

Jessie Nicoll Baillie with her grandson Alexander Baillie Ripley

*****

With Alex's transfer to Tacoma in 1888 he moved his family to a home at 14 South Tacoma Avenue, where they lived for 26 years and where all the daughters were born except Jessie, who had been born in Portland. The home overlooked Commencement Bay where Alex could see the ships coming and going. After Alex sold the home it was eventually moved and has since been torn down. The original location is now the First Presbyterian Church, which was built in 1924.

Baillie home at 14 South Tacoma Avenue

Alex had a Pierce Arrow touring car for many years and he had a chauffeur, Wilson, who was with Alex for 30 years.

Alex, with friends and Wilson driving in the Pierce Arrow. This is in front of their Tacoma house around 1909.

A charming Midsummer dance was given by Mrs. Alexander Baillie at her residence on S. Tacoma Ave., Tuesday in honor of Mrs. Burns of Portland. Guests were present from Seattle and other out-of-town cities, and the cool weather experienced Tuesday evening made the affair a social treat.- Seattle Times July 28, 1901.

While the season at Lake Cushman has opened late it looks now as if both hotels and every available camping ground will be occupied by the beginning of next week. There will be an illumination of the grounds and gardens surrounding the Antlers on Saturday evening next and these will be continued from now until the close of the season. Recent arrivals at the Antlers include the following: Alexander Baillie, Mrs. Alexander

Baillie, Ms. J Baillie, Miss A Baillie, Miss E Baillie, Miss K Baillie, Miss M Baillie, of Tacoma. - Seattle Times July 25 1904.

The Antlers Hotel, which was built at Lake Cushman in 1895, was submerged when the dam was built in 1925.

Antlers Hotel at Lake Cushman.

The social session of the Aloha Club held at the home of Mr. and Mrs. Alexander Baillie Tuesday evening was the occasion of a notable society gathering and marked the close of the club season. The final meeting of the Aloha club has for years been made an event of unusual interest in society circles and the affair of Tuesday night was strictly in keeping with that custom. The nature of the program was kept a secret until the members and their guests were assembled in the beautiful parlor of the Baillie home. – Seattle Times May 14, 1905.

The Aloha Club was founded in 1892 as a women's study club focused on promoting cultural life of the community.

One block behind the house was Wright Park, which had been established in 1890. Wright Park is 27 acres, has a very nice conservatory, pond and is planted with 100 different native and exotic trees. The Baillie family undoubtedly spent many hours playing there. Unfortunately there is this item from the newspaper:

Mrs. Alexander Baillie and daughters, Kathleen and Marian, suffered injuries when their carriage upset in Wright Park. The accident occurred when the horse drawing the carriage became alarmed at an automobile driven near it. The horse bolted, and the carriage upset.- Tacoma News Tribune September 13, 1904.

Alex Starts Tacoma Country Club, 1894 - 1900

- **1896** – Klondike Gold Rush starts
    - X-rays discovered
    - First modern Olympics
- **1898** – Spanish- American War declared
- **1899** – Aspirin patented

In Alex's office at the Balfour Guthrie and Company of Tacoma were 30 people, half of whom were homesick Scots. Many had formed cricket teams, which was a good outlet for them. But Alex felt he could relieve some of their homesickness if he could establish in Tacoma another game which so many of them had played in Scotland. Golf was played on a very informal basis wherever an open area could be found, and discussions of a club continued during the early 1890s. Finally, at the age of 35 in 1894, Alex started the Tacoma Country Club, the oldest U.S. golf club west of the Mississippi. This was the start of what would lead Alex to be known as "the father of golf in the West".

The first course was in Frederick and Rose Eisenbei's cow pasture in Edison, which is now South Tacoma. Alex leased the 280 acre pasture for $1 a year. The initiation fee for the club was set at $2.50 and the dues at $.25 per month. Alex was the first president of the club. Rose Eisenbei would serve the golfers lunch of a pot of beans or pancakes for 25 cents. When she raised the price by a nickel the frugal Scotsmen of course protested.

The clubhouse was formed by four red shingle buildings.

Original 4 Tacoma Country Club buildings

One building is where the Eisenbeis family lived, another was the club room, and the other two served as locker rooms for the men and women. Alex with a fellow Scot laid out the first course using tin cans for the 9 holes. The first tournament was held on November 29, 1894, and was won by one of the charter members as there had been little interest from others in the community. The course was primitive and filled with gravel and stones. It was open to cattle who roamed the course at will. One golfer commented years later he could still recall the hollow sound of a ball thudding into a cow. If a ball was lost, play would be stopped to conduct a search due to their high value and, of course, the club being made up mostly of those frugal Scots.

This original location in South Tacoma was between the current South 72nd St and South 76th St near Junett St. I went to that area and enjoyed walking around the neighborhood picturing Alex and fellow club members playing golf on that primitive course. One of the original four buildings still stands at 6001 Junett St.

Alex imported from Scotland 30 sets of golf clubs (both men's and women's) made by Forgan of St. Andrews and 25 dozen golf balls made of the dried gum of Malaysian Sapadilla trees. When the golf clubs arrived in Tacoma the Customs officials didn't know what they were and how to classify them. When a Customs officer said to Alex that they appeared to be agricultural implements Alex replied with a smile "yes, we do dig with them" and so classified them as such. The lower tariff on agricultural implements of course delighted Alex.

In 1896 Sir Robert Balfour of the Balfour Guthrie Company came to visit Alex and see the company operations in Tacoma. He was an ardent golfer and was so impressed that on his return to Scotland he had a gold St. Andrews medal made for the Tacoma Golf Club. This became an award used for the club championship winner starting in 1898. It has been awarded every year since except for the 28-year period from 1910 to 1938 when the medal had been lost. It was found buried in some old records in the club's safe. The medal is now briefly put around the winner's neck and then soon returned to the safe. Inscribed above the crest of the medal are the words "Far and Sure".

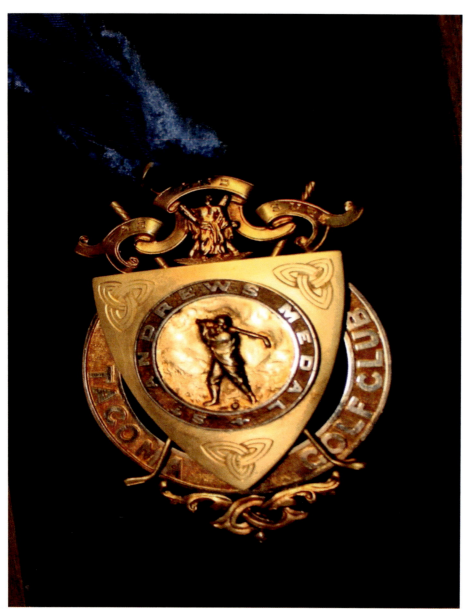
St Andrews Medal

In 1904 the club bought R.B. Lehman's 167-acre farm, which is the current Tacoma Country Club property on the north end of American Lake. They built a log cabin to serve as the club house. The log cabin burned down in 1909 and was replaced in 1910 by a club house known as the "Grand Old Lady of Lakewood" which in 1961 also burned down. The current club house was completed in 1964.

Officers for the ensuing year were elected last night at the annual meeting of the Tacoma Golf Club. The reports indicated that never before were the organization's prospects so flattering, and there was an enthusiasm displayed that augurs well for the future, Officers selected were Alexander Baillie, President; H. J. Bremmer, Secretary and Treasurer....It was decided that all old members in good standing and all new members applying before November 1 will be elected without the regular initiation fees of $25. However, after that date the fee will be necessary in order to gain admission. - Seattle Times October 5, 1905

Name over entrance to the Alexander Baillie Room at the current clubhouse

Entrance to the Alexander Baillie Room

Alex also encouraged the start of golf in Seattle, and around 1895 or 1896 five holes were created in a meadow near the Stone Way area. The sport was slow to get started there as not long afterwards many of the golfers started heading north during the Klondike gold rush.

It is interesting that at the time Alex started the club he was not really a golfer. His main athletic interests as a youth were football (soccer), tennis and cricket. He also had curling stones so I believe that also was one of his activities.

Alex's curling stone and a carrying basket

But Alex had seen golf played and thought it would be an interesting pastime for his friends. It was actually his wife Jessie, an athletic woman, who encouraged Alex to pursue introducing the game of golf. He said "To be perfectly truthful, I might have forgotten about the whole thing, but she wouldn't let me". Through the continued encouragement of Jessie and Alex's Scottish friends the whole project got started. He was 35 when he played his first real game of golf and it was 19 years before he attained his all-time best score of 80. Alex felt "Americans and Scotsmen make the best golfers – they're daring, while the English are too conservative to take chances".

It didn't take long for Alex to become an ardent golfer. He would regularly ride his bike from the home at 14 South Tacoma Ave to the golf course to get in a game with friends. The distance was about 7 miles which he covered in 45 minutes over the dirt roads and trails. His average game score for many years was between 90 and 100 which wasn't bad considering the equipment and course conditions of the time. He continued to play until his 80th birthday in 1939 when he said he "formally retired". In reality he had continued to occasionally play just hadn't been on the course with anyone else. He said he had actually gotten around the front 9 at the country club in "surprisingly few strokes – so few that no one would believe me if I told my exact score, but that's the penalty of playing alone". In his later years Alex took delight in exercising his prerogative of a man his age – "now I just follow the fellows around and criticize the way they play". He had even gone part way around the course a few months before he died. He had said in 1948 that he realized that "his decision to "retire" from golf at 80 had been a bit hasty". "Next summer, just as soon as I am 90, I am going to start in all over again – I feel that good".

This certificate number 1 was issued to Alex in 1945. Certificates were issued at the time to members at $300 each in order to raise money for improvements to the golf course.

The Daily Colonist.

(ESTABLISHED 1858)

VICTORIA, BRITISH COLUMBIA, TUESDAY, AUGUST 12, 1947

Veteran Northwest Golfers Pictured at Annual Meet

ROYAL Colwood Golf Club was one of the busiest spots on Vancouver Island yesterday as 166 veteran golfers from all parts of the Pacific Northwest teed off in the annual tournament of the Seniors' Northwest Golf Association. Always a gala occasion for the oldsters of the fairway, this year's event bids fair to be one of the most successful. In the above photo are a quintette of real old-timers. From left to right, they are: Harry Bloedel, Seattle, 83; Don Campbell, Bellingham, 81; Alex Baillie, Tacoma, 88; Raymond Frazier, Seattle, 74, and E. J. Roberts, Spokane, the oldest entrant, who admits to 90 years. Baillie and Bloedel were among the founders of the association and have been attending the annual tournaments since its inception in 1923. This is Campbell's 24th year, Roberts' 22nd and Frazier's 19th year of competition.

Alex, in center, at the age of 88 at Royal Colwood Golf Club, Victoria, British Columbia, for the annual Seniors Northwest Golf Association tournament. As noted in the article, Alex was one of the founders of the Northwest Golf Association.

Another interesting golf connection was Alex's son in law Charles H. Banks, who was married to Agnes Baillie. A Yale graduate, Charles Banks taught English and coached track at his prep school, Hotchkiss, in Connecticut for 15 years. It was there that Charles met Seth Raynor, a well-known golf course designer, who was rebuilding the school's golf course. After working on the project with Raynor, Banks quit his job at Hotchkiss in 1921 to join Raynor's firm, whose offices were in New York City. He worked with Raynor and C.B. Macdonald for five years, supervising construction of Yale Golf Club and Mid-Ocean in Bermuda, among others. When Raynor died in 1926, Banks completed 10 unfinished projects. He then designed and remodeled nearly 30 other courses in the next five years, before unexpectedly dying of a heart attack in 1931 at the age of 48. His nickname was "Steam Shovel" Banks, for he often used steam shovels to move massive amounts of earth in creating huge elevated greens and deep bunkers. That style is most evident at his designs of Whippoorwill in New York, Forsgate and The Knoll in New Jersey and Castle Harbour in Bermuda. In his work, Banks continued the Macdonald/Raynor tradition of adapting famous holes in each project. One of his favorites was the Redan, the legendary par-3 15th of Scotland's North Berwick Golf Links.

CHARLES H. BANKS
GOLF COURSE DESIGN AND CONSTRUCTION
ASSOCIATE OF THE LATE SETH J. RAYNOR

Courses now under construction:

Essex County Country Club, West Orange, N. J.
Knollwood Country Club, White Plains, N. Y.
Fairyland Golf Course, Chattanooga, Tenn.
Kinderkamack Golf Club, Hackensack, N. J.

Cavalier Hotel Golf Course, Virginia Beach, Va.
Territorial Hotel Course, Honolulu, T. H.
Rock Spring Country Club, West Orange, N. J.
Essex County Park Course, Belleville, N. J.

Other courses recently completed

331 Madison Avenue, New York City   Telephone: Murray Hill 10163

Alex and the Balfour Guthrie Company prosper, 1900 – 1928

- **1901** - President Mckinley assassinated
- **1906** - San Francisco earthquake and fire kills 4000. Balfour Guthrie offices destroyed
- **1908** - First Model T introduced
- **1909** - Alaska-Yukon-Pacific Exposition in Seattle
- **1912** - Titanic Sinks
- **1914** - First electric traffic light
- **1914 - 1918** World War I
- **1927** - Lindbergh flies across the Atlantic
- **1927** - Last Model T made (15 million)

Having lived in the United States for 18 years Alex believed it was time to become a citizen. So on January 12, 1898, in Tacoma, WA Alex became a U.S. citizen.

RECORD OF NATURALIZATION.

United States District Court, District of Washington.

In the Matter of the Application of *Alexander Baillie* **An Alien, To Become a Citizen of the United States of America.** **In open Court, this** *12th* **day of** *January* 189*8*.

It appearing to the satisfaction of this Court, by the oaths of *H. J. Brenner* and *Jas Gillison, Jr.* citizens of the United States of America, witnesses for that purpose, first duly sworn and examined, that *Alexander Baillie* a native of *Scotland* has resided within the limits and under the jurisdiction of the United States five years at least, last past; and within the State of Washington for one year at least, last past; and that during all of said time he has behaved as a man of good moral character; that he is attached to the principles of the Constitution of the United States, and well disposed to the good order and happiness of the same; and it also appearing to the Court, by competent evidence, that the said applicant has heretofore, and more than two years since, and in due form of law, declared his intention to become a citizen of the United States, and now having here, before this Court, taken an oath that he will support the Constitution of the United States of America, and that he doth absolutely and entirely renounce and adjure all allegiance and fidelity to every foreign Prince, Potentate, State or Sovereignty whatsoever, and particularly to *Victoria Queen of Great Britain and Ireland*

It is therefore ordered, adjudged and decreed by the Court that the said *Alexander Baillie* be and is hereby admitted and declared to be a citizen of the United States of America.

Enter:

_____
U. S. District Judge, District of Washington.

In 1887, while Alex was still in Portland, he had been asked to determine the best location for a new Balfour Guthrie office on Puget Sound. After a thorough study, Alex wrote up a 20-page report recommending Tacoma as the site for the new office. This led to Alex being sent the next year to open the new office.

When Alex came to Tacoma in 1888, Washington was still a territory and wouldn't become a state until the following year. There were only a few thousand people in Tacoma at that time but Alex envisioned the same long docks that he remembered from Glasgow and Liverpool. Tacoma had been chosen as the western terminus for the northern route of the transcontinental railroad by the Northern Pacific Company. Tacoma had gained the reputation as "the city of destiny". The whole area was experiencing a lot of growth and Tacoma's population grew from around 2000 in 1880 to over 20,000 in 1889.

In Tacoma Alex was a founding member of the Union Club, belonged to the Commercial Club and the Tacoma Golf and Country Club which all provided both social and business contacts. The Union Club was formed in the summer of 1888 by a number of prominent Tacoma Businessmen and the original club house was built soon after that overlooking Commencement Bay. The Union Club hosted many special guests over the years including President William Howard Taft in 1909. The Union Club no longer exists but the club house still stands at 539 Broadway.

Union club in 1891 and 1939

Balfour Guthrie Company's office in Tacoma continued to grow under Alex's leadership. Alec Williamson, the third son of Stephen Williamson, a founding partner of the Liverpool company, had been sent to Tacoma to assist Alex in establishing this new location. Alec was only there for a couple of years before moving to the main office in San Francisco. Within a few years Alex had established his office in number 202 in the Fidelity Building at 949 Broadway. The office gave him a view of the waterfront although his preference was to be down at the docks with the ships and warehouses. The Fidelity Building was built in 1890, two years after Alex arrived in Tacoma, and was torn down in 1949, the same year he died.

Alex in his Balfour Guthrie office. Note 2 phones. The panorama on the wall behind him is of the "mile long" wheat warehouses on the Tacoma waterfront.

Tacoma Seamen's Friend Society.

To carry forward the Bethel Work of this Society among the thousands of Seamen coming to this port as crews of ships to bear to the markets of the world our millions of bushels of grain, and large output of flour, coals and lumber, we ask our citizens to supply us $400.00 for the year's expenses.

With this small sum to pay for lights, fuel, rent and incidental expenses of repairs and janitor work we can do a much needed work on the water-front.

Gentlemen paying 20c. per month for the year will be constituted annual members, entitled to vote, hold office, etc., smaller sums gratefully received. For Ladies, 10c. per month.

All Subscriptions will be duly reported at the regular annual meeting, by our General Agent, Chaplain Stubbs.

We heartily commend this important mission to the confidence and sympathy of our people, especially in view of the economy of its management, and of its efficiency.

ALEX. BAILLIE, President,
THOMAS KERR,
P. V. CAESAR
J. W. VIANT,
C. W. MORRILL,
W. B. BLACKWELL,
} Officers of the T. S. F. Society.

Sept 1 1899

The company was the first to load a ship, the *Dakota*, at Tacoma with wheat in 1881 bound for Liverpool. Eventually at times there were 30 sailing ships in the Commencement Bay harbor loading or waiting to load cargo that would go all over the world. This was a scene which Alex said he would never forget. By the early 1900s Tacoma had the longest wheat warehouse complex in the world, said to be a mile long. The Balfour Guthrie warehouse was a major part of that complex. The Balfour warehouse is the only part that still remains. It has been restored and is currently Tacoma's Foss Waterway Seaport.

The British steamships Harpalyee and Aberiour are due here to load wheat for the United Kingdom and the continent, the former taking 9000 tons and the latter 7000. Announcement to this effect was made today by Alexander Baillie resident partner of Balfour Guthrie and Company. The Norwegian steamship Sommerstad, also under charter to the Balfour Guthrie Company will arrive soon to load wheat at Seattle and Tacoma. She will carry approximately 4000 tons. The vessel was employed last summer in the Alaskan waters as a whaler.- Seattle Times October 27 1912.

Balfour Guthrie & Co was also involved in whaling. A September 13, 1911, article in the Seattle Times announced that Alexander Baillie had issued contracts to the Moran Company of Seattle to build "three steam whalers, oil-burning, and built of steel". These whalers were to operate in the North Pacific off the coast of Washington, British Columbia and Alaska. The total cost of the three ships was about $185,000.

It is interesting how diversified Balfour Guthrie & Co became. In Portland they provided financing to farmers, eventually creating a subsidiary to handle these transactions. They also got involved in the cleaning and classification of grain, plus marine insurance. According to the Balfour Guthrie & Co history it was their involvement with coal and iron ore mining in the Washington Cascades that spurred the opening of the Tacoma office. In the Northwest they were involved in cement production in Bellingham and flour milling in Portland. There were also numerous agricultural and land development interests, mostly in California. But the biggest and most successful investment was in the newly discovered oil industry in California between San Francisco and Los Angeles. Balfour Guthrie set up two companies to buy land near where oil had been discovered, Aetna Petroleum Company and Avenal Land and Oil Company. Numerous wells were drilled on the properties but unfortunately they were all dry. Balfour Guthrie was not to be deterred and after careful investigation of some new land near Coalinga they created a third company called California Oilfields Limited and bought more land. By the end of 1901 several rich wells had come in without a single failure. Soon they built Balfour Town for the comfort of the field staff that included housing and stores. Within eight years of incorporation California Oilfields was the biggest oil producer in California. In 1913 California Oilfields was sold to Shell Oil.

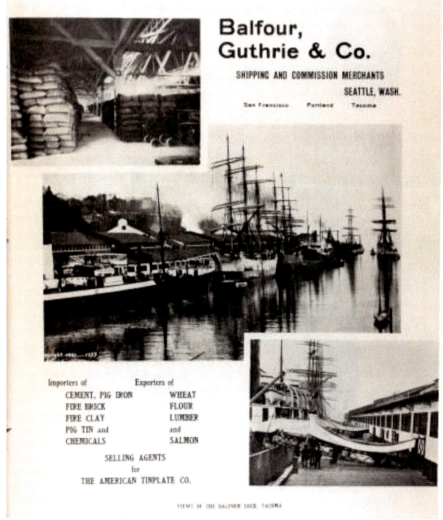

Balfour Guthrie Co ad from 1904

Alex was also busy with many activities outside but related to his job with the company. A legal entry in the April 24, 1911, Seattle Times shows a notarized acceptance by the Insurance Commissioner of the State of Washington of Alexander Baillie as Attorney in Fact for British and Foreign Marine Insurance Company Ltd of Liverpool.

In June 1914 Alex presented a report to the first annual conference of the Pacific Coast Association of Port Authorities that was held in Seattle. The conference was focused on port problems throughout the United States.

On November 20, 1914, Alex gave a luncheon in recognition of Russian trade:
"The people of Seattle don't fully realize the importance of the Russian volunteer fleets new service between the North Pacific and Russia" said Alexander Baillie resident partner of Balfour Guthrie and Company at a luncheon which he gave yesterday in the Rainier Club in honor of the inauguration of the service. "Russia's trade with Germany alone last year", he continued," reached the enormous sum of $337 million and because of the European war this country is now to get a share of that commerce. The Russians are large importers of machinery and manufactured goods which will now move in heavy quantities by way of Seattle and North Pacific ports". Nicholas Bogolavlensky, Russian Consul in Seattle, was the guest of honor at the banquet. The other guests were prominent Seattle bankers and businessmen. – Seattle Times November 21 1914

Alex was on the marine transportation and port development committee, which was part of the Chamber of Commerce. The committee handles all matters pertaining to water transportation, especially those that grow out of the import and export business with which the foreign trade bureau had to deal.

In November 1917 Alex was appointed head of the Fuel Oil Committee by the federal fuel administrator in Washington, DC. The state was facing a serious fuel situation, and the committee was to investigate present receipts of fuel oil, possible increases, a survey of the amount of oil used for various purposes, and of the possibility in each case of substituting some more easily attainable fuel. Recommendations may include priority delivery to certain industries considered most necessary to the conduct of the war. In 1919, after the war, Alex was on the Chamber of Commerce committee to investigate excessive oil prices being charged Pacific Coast steamships since the end of WW I by the major oil companies.

*****

In 1907 Alex became a partner in the company and eventually senior partner. In October of 1914 Alex and Jessie moved their family to Seattle soon after Balfour Guthrie's northwest headquarters had been moved there. They first lived at the Washington Hotel for about a year. They later moved to a home in the Seattle Highlands known as Glen Kerry, which was owned by Mr. and Mrs. A. S. Kerry who were away on an extended trip.

This picture was taken in front of Glenn Kerry around 1915. Back row: Mr. Walter Burns (Senior partner Balfour Guthrie Co.), Jessie Baillie, Alex, Marian Baillie, Agnes (Polly) Banks, Charles Banks, Kathleen Baillie, Billie Ripley. Middle row: Sam Russell, Lee Russell, Jessie Ripley. Front row: Mac (the dog), Bill Johnson, Alec Ripley.

Glenn Kerry in the Seattle Highlands

It was 1916 when Alex purchased and moved his family to a 15,000-square-foot mansion at 907 14th Ave East Seattle. The mansion had been built in 1912 by Samuel S Loeb, a contemporary of Alex's and the president of the Milwaukee Brewing Company of Tacoma. The home had cost Mr. Loeb about $150,000 to build. Mr. Loeb had come to Tacoma the year after Alex. The home had 20 rooms including a ballroom with a pipe organ that was described as a "notably fine one". An article in the Seattle times called the home "one of the finest residence properties in the city". At the time it was one of the few solid brick homes in the city. The floors were covered with rugs woven in Ireland. Census reports show that Alex had maids and a cook who lived in the mansion. Alex lived there for about 10 years but sold the home to Julius Shafer of the Shafer Bros Land Company in 1927 and moved back to Tacoma in 1929. The home is currently the Shafer Baillie Mansion Bed and Breakfast.

Pictures of the Baillie mansion in Seattle

Baillie mansion in Seattle

In Seattle, Alex was a member of the Rainier Club, The Metropolitan Club, the Seattle Golf and Country Club (he was elected trustee in 1919), the Seattle Tennis Club, and the Chamber of Commerce. He also was an active member of St Mark's Episcopal Church.

He served on the board, was Vice Chairman and on the Executive Committee for membership of the Seattle chapter of the American Red Cross. During a major fundraiser in Seattle Alex was a committee capt. and signed a fund-raising letter that read in part as follows:

The Red Cross is the product of wisdom and experience and represents the best thoughts of our time. It is prompt, sympathetic, scientific and efficient. No other agency can accomplish this vast humanitarian work. It will be our fault if this fails through lack of funds. We therefore urge upon every man woman and child in Seattle to do his or her utmost and to make a dutiful and liberal response to the President's appeal. Remember a soldier is either a member of your family or your neighbors. Do not neglect him in his dire need. - Seattle Times June 10, 1917.

Alex was Vice Chairman of the executive committee of the "Gigantic Carnival, Amusement City and Bazaar" that was put on in Seattle to raise money for the war relief in 1917. The goal was to raise $100,000 with half going to equip base hospital #50 behind the lines in France and the rest going to the local Red Cross civilian relief. In the same year Alex was also on the Industry Committee that supported the sale of $36 million in Liberty Bonds in the state of Washington.

In 1917 Alex was one of four committee members chosen to select the location for the headquarters of the British recruiting office in Seattle. In the same year he was also appointed a Director of the Associated Charities of Seattle, which provided assistance to the poor.

Alex was a member of the British - American Association and in 1923 was elected Vice Chairman. The Association grew out of the British American Relief Association during World War I and continued to provide welfare work to needy British soldiers and their families in Seattle.

Alex was elected as Vice President of the Rainier Club in 1925. He was president of the Club from 1926 – 1927. In 1927 he was named chairman of the building committee at a time when the Rainier club was just starting on a $500,000 expansion.

Joshua Greene, Seattle capitalist, last night succeeded Alexander Baillie as president of the Rainier club at the annual dinner meeting of the membership which followed the election of officers for the next 12 months. Mr. Baillie presided at the meeting and in accordance with the time honored custom turned over the gavel to Mr. Green, the new president. Then Mr. Baillie was presented a gift from the members as a token of his leadership during the last year.- Seattle Times Oct 16, 1927.

Photos of Rainier Club presidents at this time were being taken by Edward Curtis, a very well-known photographer who had a studio in Seattle.

Alex as Rainier Club president. Photographer Edward Curtis's signature is in lower right corner.

The first of the elm trees with which it is proposed to line Memorial way, or the highway from Seattle to Tacoma, were planted at the edge of the city limits by Gold Star Mothers, members of the Garden Club, American Legion, and public spirited citizens. When the plans are completed it is hoped that the Seattle Tacoma highway will be an avenue of 2700 elm trees space at 60 foot distances. Those who planted trees yesterday include Mr. Alexander Baillie.....- Seattle Times November 12, 1921.

This memorial was to honor those who had lost their lives during WW I and had been spearheaded by the Seattle Garden Club. Some of the trees that were planted are still visible particularly in Des Moines on Memorial Way.

In 1922 Alex was on the advisory committee for the "New Seattle Hotel". This hotel would become the Olympic Hotel which was completed in 1924 and is now known as the Fairmont.

In 1929 Alex was the Treasurer of the Washington State Society for the Conservation of Wildflowers and Tree Planting. This society had been started in 1927 by Mrs. Alexander (Lillian) F. McEwan, a close friend of the Baillie's, who was very active in society and conservation and in 1917 had founded the Seattle Garden Club.

In 1930 Alex and second wife Ida were appointed to the national committee to decide on an appropriate memorial to Stephen T. Mather, the first director of the National Park Service, who had died earlier that year. Mather had been instrumental in the development of Mount Rainier National Park. There is currently the Mather Memorial Highway that runs from the north entrance to Mount Rainier National Park up to Chinook Pass.

When Balfour Guthrie became a Corporation on January 1, 1930, Alex became the first president. After 52 years in the shipping trade he retired from Balfour Guthrie Company on August 10, 1931. At the time of his retirement he was the longest serving employee of the company. On October 18th, 1931 the Seattle Times ran a story on Alexander Baillie and his views on the future of the Seattle port. When he first came to the Northwest he could envision both Tacoma and Seattle becoming great shipping ports. He shared his vision with his employer, the Balfour Guthrie & Co. and they supported the growth of both Alex and the company in the area. In the article he is quoted as saying "I regard Seattle as the most important American port of the North Pacific and it will continue to be. There is no need to fear Vancouver or Tacoma or Portland. They will never be Seattle's competitors. As far as any shipping line favoring San Francisco that is all posh and tosh" according to Mr. Baillie "Whenever a shipping line is going to make 50 cents by giving Seattle more service they'll do it before you can say Jack Robinson". Alex said "people pull for their home town until it pulls something out of their pocket". Alex believed that in order for Seattle to continue to grow as a port they needed to be more internationally minded and we should study the wants of other countries particularly in the Orient. He felt that Seattle needed to focus on items that were distributed from Seattle and that were not just passing through the port. He gave examples of products such as sugar which was best refined in the Philippines but could be distributed in Seattle "for a pretty penny". Another example he gave was hemp which he felt could best be manufactured into rope in Seattle due to the need for intricate machinery and a higher class of labor. A third example was copra which is the white meat inside a coconut. It is used for oil and the refuse is made into cattle feed. "Why there has never been any mills for extracting the oil from copra established in Seattle I can't understand". He went on to say "Seattle's development as a port has been one of the marvels of this country." He said with pride. "Nothing can hold it back. A port doesn't need to seek commerce. Commerce seeks the port when the need arises. All we have to do is be ready." He felt that Seattle's facilities were A-1 and the city is full of businessmen who are "up on their toes". The writer of the article said that although he is a man of worldwide influence and assuredly one of the great shipping powers in this country he has a simple way of expressing himself. When he laughs he laughs heartily, throwing back his head and tipping backward in his swivel chair. At the time of the article Alex had recently retired from Balfour Guthrie and Company but he continued to report almost daily to either the Seattle or Tacoma offices and was still acting in an advisory capacity.

While living in Seattle Alex's wife Jessie was active in the community as she had been in Tacoma. In Seattle she was prominent in the Sunset Club, the Seattle Garden Club, and parish work at St Mark's Cathedral. She was an active supporter of the Children's Orthopedic Hospital. She was also a member of the Seattle Golf Club and the Seattle Tennis Club. She was actively involved with the YWCA, where she served on committees to raise funds to support those involved with WW I activities. She was also a patroness for the Seattle Association for the Blind and Lighthouse for Blind. Jessie was the "sponsor" for the building of the steamship *Birriwa* which was built for the Australian government by the Patterson MacDonald ship builders of Seattle. A picture in the June 28, 1918, Seattle Times shows Jessie christening the ship. Jessie was on the executive committee of the local WSS (war savings stamps) Metal Market where she was in charge of the stamps. The WSSMM collected precious metals in exchange for the war savings stamps. This was to raise funds for the war effort and provide precious metals needed for manufacturing. Jessie was also active in hosting teas during golf tournaments that raised funds for war relief.

*****

Alex and Jessie had a very active social life in both Tacoma and Seattle giving dinners, luncheons, teas, and fund raisers. There are 880 references to Alexander Baillie in the Seattle Times, many of which are social activities.

The following are just a few examples:

A delightful bowling party was given at the Union club Wednesday evening by Mr. and Mrs. T.B. Wallace in honor of Mr. and Mrs. Alexander Baillie, who've returned from an extended European trip. A delicious supper was served by the club's chef. – Seattle Times November 2 1902

One of the largest and most elaborate receptions of the summer season was that given Wednesday afternoon by Mrs. Alexander Baillie to introduce her daughter, Miss Agnes Lindsay Baillie, one of the season's most charming debutantes. Mr. and Mrs. Baillie followed the reception with a ball in honor of their daughter Thursday evening at the Union club.-Seattle Times August 25, 1907.

Mrs. Alexander Baillie and daughter Miss Marion Baillie, who have been in California for several months, will return the end of the week.- Seattle Times February 23, 1916. A February 13, 1916 article said they were at the Hotel Del Coronado at which there had been presented "An Afternoon in Japan" with special Japanese dances and soloists who gave selections from "Madame Butterfly". Tea was served by members of the "younger set" in Japanese costumes. The proceeds of the affair went to the Helping Hands Home in San Diego. A picture with the article shows Marian Baillie in a Japanese costume.

With a packed house, the glitter of gold and gems, and music golden in every sense of the word, the short season of grand Opera began at the Moore Theatre. L'Amore Dei Tre Re", given here for the first time, was the opera selected for the opening night. It drew a brilliant and large audience, one which donned its best "bib and tucker" to do honor to the occasion. The boxes with many of the leaders of society in gorgeous gowns and jewels, made a magnificent picture, which was true of the entire house, for row after row from the orchestra back presented a panorama of beauty. Among those who entertained last evening with box parties were Mr. and Mrs. Alexander Baillie, who had as their guests Mr. and Mrs. Samuel L Russell, Miss Marion Baillie, and Mrs. William Barrett, of Portland. Seattle Times March 28, 1916.

The entertainment plan for next week will feature prominent girl speakers. They have been in France with Red Cross workers for several months and only recently returned. Each will tell in her own way the experience of the trip. Another delightful feature of the evening will be the opportunity of hearing pipe organ selections by well-known organist of the city. The affair will take place in the ballroom of the Alexander Baillie residence. At the close of the entertainment a silver collection will be taken for the Children's Orthopedic Hospital. - The Seattle Times June 3 1919.

Dr. H. G. Bueller (Headmaster) of Hotchkiss School in Lakeville Connecticut, and Mrs. Bueller, motored down with Alexander Baillie and his daughter, Mrs. Charles Banks from Vancouver BC. Mr. and Mrs. Baillie entertained with a small dinner at the Sunset club. A motor trip to Mount Rainier was another enjoyable feature of their stay. – Seattle Times August 17, 1919

The two card parties, Tuesday and Wednesday, at the home of Mrs. Alexander Baillie, for the benefit of the Lighthouse for the blind, are a center of interest just now. - Seattle Times November 7 1920.

Thursday Evening Mr. and Mrs. Alexander Baillie had a small dinner for Admiral and Mrs. Eberle at their home. Admiral Edward Eberle is the Commander of the Pacific Fleet. - Seattle Times August 7 1921.

In the July 31, 1921 Seattle Times there is a picture of Admiral and Mrs. Eberle with Alex and Jessie in their Pierce Arrow car up at Paradise on Mt. Rainier.

Thursday evening Sir Auckland (British Ambassador) and Lady Geddes were the guests of honor at a dinner of 14 covers given by Mr. and Mrs.

Alexander Baillie at their home. Seattle Times April 2, 1922. The Baillie's had been guests the previous evening at a dinner at the Sunset Club in honor of the British Ambassador.

Admiral and Mrs. Eberle will be guests of Mr. and Mrs. Alexander Baillie on a three day motor trip up Hood Canal and to Vancouver Island leaving town next Friday morning. – Seattle Times August 4, 1922.

Obviously quite the most important event close by is the Admirals Ball Tuesday evening at Paradise Inn in Mount Rainier National Park. The Inn is preparing for the gayest day or so in its history..... The senior officers of the Pacific Fleet will be the guests of the reception committee for the trip........ the reception committee includes Mr. and Mrs. Alexander Baillie.....- Seattle Times August 6 1922.

The second in the interesting series of twilight musicales arranged by Mrs. Frederick Bentley under the auspices of the Woman's Council of St Mark's Church will be given at 4:00 o'clock Sunday afternoon, January 28th, in the ballroom of Mr. and Mrs. Alexander Baillie' home....The first of the musicales, early in December at the Alexander Baillie residence, was a notable success, promising much for the others to follow. Seattle Times, January 14, 1923.

To honor Mrs. Coontz, wife of Admiral Robert E Coontz, commander in chief of the United States Navy, Mrs. Alexander Baillie will entertain with a luncheon at her home on Tuesday Afternoon. – Seattle Times August 15 1924.

When Adrian Gips, Managing Director of the Holland America Line, came to Seattle in 1927 he was entertained at a luncheon at the Rainier Club. *Alexander Baillie, resident partner of the Balfour Guthrie Company, was the toastmaster. The guests included more than a score of prominent shipping and waterfront men of Seattle and Tacoma* – Seattle Times May 8, 1927.

Favored guests at the luncheon which Mr. and Mrs. R. P. Butchart of Victoria B.C. gave yesterday and compliment to Their Majesties, the King and Queen of Siam were Mr. and Mrs. John W Eddy of Seattle and

Mr. and Mrs. Alexander Baillie of Tacoma. The luncheon tables in the famous Butchart Gardens held special arrangements of flowers, that of the royal party having a motif of blue and pink. Seattle Times September 12, 1931.

*****

Sadly, in 1926, while they were living in Seattle, Jessie, died at the age of 65. She died at home surrounded by Alex and her five daughters. It is unclear what she died of but she had been sick for some time and her death had been expected for several days. Jessie is buried in the Tacoma Cemetery. Alex donated $2500 to the Seattle Children's Orthopedic Hospital in Jessie's memory for an endowed room.

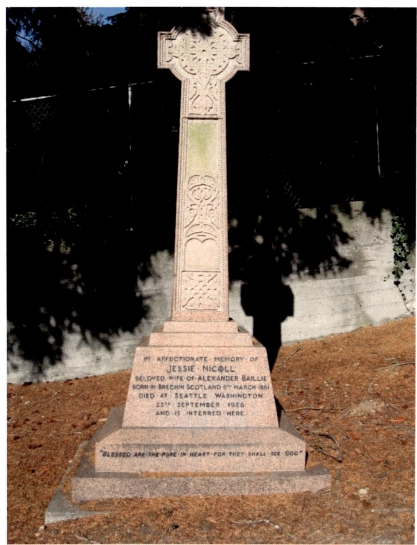
Jessie Nicoll Baillie's gravestone

Inscription on Jessie Nicoll Baillie's gravestone

*****

From the moment Alex arrived in Tacoma, way back in 1888, Mount Rainier was always a part of his life. Early on it was something that he would just see in the distance from his home on South Tacoma Ave or down on the Tacoma waterfront. But later it became a destination for many enjoyable trips and he would become part of a company that played a prominent role in the development of the park.

Mount Rainier National Park was created in 1899. Interest in the park and access to it continued to grow in the early 1900s. In 1907 automobiles were allowed into the park up to Longmire. To decide how to manage the growth the Rainier National Park Advisory Committee was formed made up of interested people from the Tacoma and Seattle area. In 1915 Steven T. Mather, Assistant Secretary of the Interior in charge of National Parks, met with the Rainier National Park Advisory Committee in Seattle to plan a more efficient system for tourist services and accommodations. At the time the committee consisted of T.H. Martin, Chester Thorne, H.A. Rhodes, Alex Baillie, William Jones, S.A. Perkins, David Whitcomb, Joseph Blethen, Everett Griggs, J.B. Terns, Herman Chapin, Samuel Hill, C.D. Stimson. Mather conducted an eighty-five mile pack trip around the Wonderland Trail with members of the Committee and other selected commercial leaders of the two cities.

It was agreed that management of concessions within the park must be consolidated under a single company, a "regulated monopoly" as Mather called it. The local committee of Puget Sound businessmen agreed to form this company to manage the concessions. On March 1, 1916, the Rainier National Park Company (RNPC), was formed, and was granted a 20-year "preferential concession" lease by the National Park Service (NPS), which had been created the same year.

Alex was on the board of the RNPC from the beginning. In 1929 he was elected president (two years before he retired from Balfour Guthrie Co), a position he held until 1944 when he became chairman of the board. He remained chairman of the board right up to his death.

The businessmen who formed the Rainier National Park Company were naturally interested in profits like any business owners. But they were also motivated by the prospect of making Mount Rainier National Park into a nationally-renowned asset of the Pacific Northwest and a magnet for regional growth. The executives of the company took no compensation. Of RNPC's 142 stockholders in 1919, all but nine lived in Seattle or Tacoma, and all but eight were owners, executives, or general managers of businesses in the region. Alex sent the following letter to his one-year-old great grandson John Baker in 1943.

2 Nov 1943.

The Town House
LOS ANGELES

My very dear John,

Good morning with affectionate greetings from your great grand-father and I understand you have had or about to have your first birthday — well my boy as you are not quite old enough to go fishing with me & cast a fly, I thought

I would give you something you could always remember so here is the cheque for my salary as President of the Rainier National Park for last year and it would seem to me to be a good idea for you to cash this cheque & buy one dollars worth of war stamps. God bless you and with my love

Great Grandfather
Baillie

At the time RNPC started there were many concessionaires within the park and many of them were fly by night operators that provided very poor service. RNPC was able to transition to the single concession operator in just over 2 years. They built a hotel, Paradise Inn, which opened in 1917. That building as shown below had cost $91,000 to build. The RNPC set up a transportation department within the company. Three individuals who had previously operated passenger automobile service to the park, each sold their equipment to the RNPC for company stock. In the summer of 1921, the state highway director ruled that the RNPC would be the only carrier between Seattle or Tacoma and points inside Mount Rainier National Park. By 1926 there were 40 of the auto stages being operated from the two cities.

Paradise Inn and company stages. (O.A. Tomlinson Collection photo courtesy of University of Washington)

At Longmire the RNPC was able to acquire most of the private concessionaires and in the process removed the various tent stores and outbuildings thereby improved the area. The RNPC decided not to develop the Longmire Springs area and instead wanted to focus its attention on the Paradise area, where more and more visitors wanted to go. In 1920 RNPC demolished the Longmire Springs Hotel and moved an annex that had been nearby across the road and next to the National Park Inn. In 1926 the National Park Inn burned down and the Annex became the new and current National Park Inn.

The Longmire Springs area was one of the only privately owned properties remaining. In the 1930's Alex was involved in the very protracted negotiations for the NPS to buy the property from the Longmire Mineral Springs Company who had bought the property from the Longmire family. Complicating the discussions was that Alex's wife Ida owned 25 percent of the Longmire Mineral Springs Company, which led the NPS to speculate that Alex might not be negotiating in good faith. The reality was that both Ida and Alex were anxious to ensure the NPS got ownership of the property and that the natural beauty of the area was protected from uncontrolled private businesses. Finally after more than 10 years a deal was reached and the NPS took ownership in 1939.

Mount Rainier's total annual visitation grew from 34,814 visitors in 1915, to 123,708 visitors in 1923, on the way to 265,620 visitors in 1930. The first 10 years of RNPC operations proved to be successful and they were making an average net profit of 17 percent. They provided transportation, hotel, canvas-walled tent camping areas with food service, horseback trips, dogsledding, sleigh rides, tobogganing, and guide services. In 1917 Asahel Curtis, a photographer like his brother Edward Curtis, was hired as the RNPC first chief guide. They also built infrastructure, like power plants to provide electricity to their services.

But there were challenges. One of the biggest challenges was that business was very seasonal with the busiest times only during three months of summer. Many buildings were closed down and left empty during much of the year but the maintenance costs continued. As more and more people started coming by their own automobile, often just for the day, this impacted the company's business. Auto traffic grew from 70 in 1907 to 10,434 in 1919. The RNPC restrooms were the only thing the auto travelers used. Instead of staying in the canvas-walled tents of the RNPC they stayed in NPS free campgrounds and brought their own tents. As the company's officers consistently pointed out, the RNPC made its money mostly from patrons who traveled by train. These were the people who boarded the company's auto stages in Tacoma or Seattle and stayed at the Paradise Inn. By the early 30s RNPC was $375,000 in debt, and in 1933 they didn't know if they would even be able to open that summer.

As it became clearer during the latter 20s that the current business model was not sustainable other proposals were developed. More winter activities were planned, but the task of trying to keep the road open to Paradise was very challenging. There wasn't any significant growth of winter activities until the 1930s. It was during that time that skiing started to be popular in many places around the U.S. In the early 30s the road was plowed from Longmire up to Narada Falls and the visitors would hike up to Paradise. For a couple of years in the mid 30s the road was plowed all the way to Paradise. They started to have slalom and downhill races. Even Olympic ski team trials were held at Paradise. By the winter of 1937-38 Paradise was the leading ski resort in the Pacific Northwest and a rope tow had been installed along with lights for night skiing. RNPC rented out rooms at Paradise Inn and offered ski lessons that were taught by an Austrian, Otto Lang. There was even a small ski lodge built in 1941 at the peak of the skiing activity at Paradise and also the start of World War II.

But over these later years the NPS was starting to question whether skiing at Mount Rainier National Park was an appropriate activity. The NPS started to put limitations on skiing activities. This, along with World WarII, contributed to the continual decline of skiing at Paradise. RNPC was optimistic about the opportunities that winter activities, particularly skiing, offered but without more financial support they were not able to take full advantage. Additionally most of the skiers, like the summer visitors, came for the day and didn't spend much.

Plans were also made for new hotels at Yakima (Sunrise) and Spray Park, a tram from Nisqually Glacier to Paradise in order to extend the business season into the winter by creating a winter resort at Paradise, and a golf course. Some of these proposals were supported by the NPS as they wanted RNPC to succeed, but NPS didn't provide any monetary support. RNPC was hopeful it could get financing from the railroads as had happened at some of the other national parks. But the lack of out-of-state hotel visitors made the railroads reluctant to invest. Yet surprisingly, RNPC officials did manage, with help from Mather and the NPS, to interest the Northern Pacific, Great Northern, Union Pacific, and Milwaukee Road in a $2.5 million joint development proposal in 1928-29. The railroads sent investigators to the park to determine the feasibility and all came back with positive reports. But it wasn't until early 1930 that the executives of the railroads met for a final decision and at that time agreed to decline the offer. This was just as the Great Depression was starting, which probably had a significant impact on their decision.

A nine-hole golf course was the only proposal that actually became a reality, and in 1931 it opened in Paradise Valley. This was while Alex was president of RNPC so I suspect he had a hand in making that happen. But the golf course only lasted about two years.

Although proposals were significantly scaled back, the original Paradise Inn was refurbished, repainted and retained as the most luxurious hotel in the park. The tents which had surrounded it on three sides were removed. Plans for a deluxe hotel were abandoned; instead, the RNPC built 275 housekeeping cabins and a central service building with cafeteria, camp store, and 40 guest rooms. This building was called the Paradise Lodge. The housekeeping cabins and lodge were located away from the Paradise Inn. Built during the fall of 1930, the cabins and lodge were opened to the public on June 20, 1931. RNPC also was involved in the development of the Sunrise area. This was drastically scaled back from the original proposal which had included a 300-room hotel. In 1931 they ended up building 215 housekeeping cabins and a central service building containing a cafeteria, camp store, post office, storage, and employee dormitories. They started marketing this area as a dude ranch.

The failure of RNPC dreams and the NPS hopes reflected underlying weaknesses in the partnership of public and private investment in Mount Rainier National Park. When the Great Depression hit, the RNPC suffered a blow that it never fully recovered from. The reduction in visitors to the park, their reduced spending and the NPS turning its focus to the Federal Government programs during the recession all had a significant impact on the RNPC. Alex confided to a business associate, "Between you and me and the gatepost, I have been pretty much disgusted with the attitude of the National Park Service in regard to our problems, and while I am optimistic about the future of the Rainier National Park, we don't get very much help from the 'powers that be' in Washington."

In 1940 Rainier National Park Company sold its interests to the federal government but retained the right to lease all business opportunities until 1968, when the corporation was dissolved.

When Alex died he was not a wealthy man. He had been a very successful businessman with Balfour Guthrie Co., but I suspect that the combination of the depression and the financial struggles of RNPC, which he was deeply involved with, had a significant impact on his finances.

Upon Alex's resignation as president of RNPC he was sent the following letter by the directors:

RAINIER NATIONAL PARK COMPANY

General Office

TACOMA 1, WASHINGTON

Nov. 20, 1944

Mr. Alexander Baillie
Palm Springs, Calif.

Dear Mr. Baillie:

Your decision to retire from the presidency of the Rainier National Park Company was one in which we have acquiesced with great reluctance. Had it not been for the fact that we found ourselves in full sympathy with your personal reasons for relinquishing that position, we should have prevailed upon you with all the eloquence at our command to continue longer in office. For we are of one accord in the belief that no business organization could wish for a finer quality of leadership than you have provided during your tenure of office. Fortunately we can take comfort in the fact that you will remain with us as Chairman of the Board.

We could not allow the occasion of your retirement to pass without expressing to you our appreciation of the invaluable services you have rendered to the company. Your wisdom, foresight, and unerring judgment have been among its most precious assets during the years when its business fortunes were at a very low ebb. Largely through your unremitting efforts the company was brought safely through one of the most difficult periods in its history, and you may well take pride in that accomplishment.

Through your active participation in its affairs, you have won many new friends for the corporation; you have enlarged its prestige in the community, and strengthened the faith of all in its future. Within the organization itself you have inspired an intense loyalty among employees, all of whom have felt for you the deepest personal respect and admiration.

Your achievements in the interest of the company have earned the gratitude of us all, and would, by themselves, deserve the highest tribute. But we should like, each of us, to acknowledge a personal debt to you for one of the richest blessings life affords—the gift of sincere friendship. Your steadfast honesty, your good-natured tolerance of our differing viewpoints, your unwavering confidence in us, your kindly interest in our personal welfare — these things have inspired us to better efforts, and have made our association together an experience we shall treasure in memory for years to come.

For all these reasons we salute you on this occasion, and send you our unanimous wish for all happiness in the future.

Most cordially yours,

Henry A. Rhodes	William Virges
A. M. Fraser	J. L. Carman Jr.
E. G. Griggs II	L. T. Murray
S. M. Morris	F. D. Metzger
J. J. Underwood	A. H. Landram
David Whitcomb	Walter W. Frankland
Sam Barnes	Paul H. Sceva
Herbert Witherspoon	

Alex's later years 1928 – 1949

- **1928** – Scottish bacteriologist Alexander Fleming discovers Penicillin
  - Amelia Earhart first woman to fly across Atlantic
- **1929** - St Valentine's Day Massacre in Chicago
  - "Black Thursday" start of stock market crash
- **1931** – Empire State Building opens
- **1933** – Franklin D Roosevelt inaugurated as 32nd US President
- **1935** – "Black Sunday" Great dustbowl storm sweeps across US prairies
- **1936** – Adolf Hitler opens 11th Olympic Games
  - Edward VII abdicates British throne to marry Wallis Simpson
- **1939** – World War II declared
- **1945** – World War II ends
- **1946** – United Nations Security Council holds first meeting

Alex remarried at the age of 69, two years after Jessie died. He married Ida Stone Jones on September 8, 1928, at the home of Mr. and Mrs. Robert P Butchart outside of Victoria, British Columbia, in front of a small group of relatives and intimate friends. The Butcharts were close friends of Alex and Ida and made frequent visits to each other's homes over the years. Ida was the widow of William Jones, a prominent Tacoma Businessman and Whitman College benefactor. They had both grown up in Walla Walla.

Ida was a very proficient golfer. At the Tacoma Country Club she won three Women's Club Championships in '03, '10, and '12 and was runner-up in '14, '15, '17, and '20. Alex was good at promoting the game of golf but was neither a winner of the Men's Club Championship nor runner-up.

Keen interest follows word that June 10 will find senior women golfers of the Northwest as guests on the Rainier Club links, and many sticks are being rediscovered for the one hole course at the Seattle Golf Club. Mrs. Alexander Baillie is using those purchased in the 90s of famous Scotch makers, and women who played together then are promising the gallery an interesting site as they play the one hole. The trophy for this one hole was put up by Mrs. Alexander Baillie – Seattle Times May 26, 1935.

After getting married they spent a couple of months on a motor trip through Scotland and England.

Mr. and Mrs. Alexander Baillie, who've been abroad the past few months, following their marriage, reached New York City Tuesday on the Berengaria and are expected home the end of the week. They have planned to be at Waloma, in the country club colony, until they go south. – Seattle Times December 16, 1928

For the first couple of years they spent their summers in Tacoma and winters in San Francisco where they had an apartment. Later the winters were spent in Palm Springs. When in Tacoma they lived in Ida's Spanish style estate at 12718 Gravelly Lake Dr. Tacoma WA which was next to the Tacoma Country Club. This estate was known as "Waloma" derived from the combination of Walla Walla, Ida's home town, and Tacoma.

Alex and Ida at Waloma

Front Entrance to Waloma

The large gardens were designed by an English landscape architect who was connected to Butchart Gardens in Victoria, B.C. Ida and Alex often traveled to Europe and spent a lot of time in Italy. Ida often had gatherings at Waloma, sharing both those gardens and her experience visiting the gardens in Italy.

Waloma's well known gardens

Hardly had the enthusiasm of a visit to the Todd Inlet Gardens of Mr. and Mrs. R.P. Butchart grown familiar to Tacoma Garden club members before the October promise of Waloma carried on their interest. On the second Tuesday of the coming month members are invited to the American Lake home of Mr. and Mrs. Alexander Baillie for an Italian day. Besides being hostess, Mrs. Baillie will recount some of her own experiences and gardens of Italy. – Seattle Times September 15 1935.

The meeting in October 1935 at Waloma by the Tacoma Garden club was described in the Seattle Times as follows:

Beauty of greensward, of stately firs, contrasted by the vivid scarlet changing leaves, splashing water of fountains and waterfalls, rock garden steps leading far down to the shore, pools reflecting summer flowers and brilliant madrona berries, winding paths shadowed and sunlit in turn,- these made of October's meeting a remembered beauty.- Seattle Times October 14, 1935

While married to Ida they had a home in Palm Springs where they would spend the winter months. Alex called his home in Palm Springs "Life in Heaven".

On January 18, 1940 while living at their Palm Springs home they were able to attend in Los Angeles the wedding of Alex's grandson Alec Ripley to Mary Roberts. On December 4, 1948, there was a 6.3 earthquake in the Palm Springs area and Alex said it knocked him off his feet but fortunately he landed on the bed.

Alex in his highland dress at the Palm Springs home

Ida died March 9, 1944, at the age of 77 while at their Palm Springs home with Alex by her side. She had been sick for many months.

*****

After Ida died in 1944 Alex asked his oldest daughter, Jessie, to move in with him. Although Alex was in good physical and mental condition it was nice to have someone share the large house with him. Jessie's husband Billie had died in 1935 at the age of 48 so it was good for both of them to share the large house. She lived with him at Waloma until he died.

Alex traveled a lot in his life making well over 40 trips across the Atlantic. The travels were for extended periods of time often spending months in Europe or in California. Trips to California were often either by car or steamship. Trips to Europe involved a train trip across the country to New York which took 3-4 days and then steamship to Europe which was another 6 days. Alex's daughters would sometimes travel with them. There are also references to both Marian and Kathleen spending a week or two at Eaton Ranch, which is a dude ranch in north central Wyoming and is still in operation.

Here are some newspaper references to some of Alex's and his family's travels:

Alexander Baillie of Balfour Guthrie and Company leaves today for London. He will remain in Europe three or four months. - Seattle Times February 2 1902.

Mr. and Mrs. Alexander Baillie and three daughters, the misses Jessie, Agnes, and Elizabeth, left yesterday for the East, to sail from there to Europe. After a brief visit in Scotland a tour of the Continent will be made. Mr. and Mrs. Baillie will place their daughters in school before returning to Tacoma.- Seattle Times February 23, 1902. The reference to placing the girls in school is unclear but I believe they went to the Hotchkiss School in Connecticut.

A number of people from the north are sojourning in California. Among the Seattle guests who were at the Hotel Del Monte, Monterey, are Mr. and Mrs. Alexander Baillie and their daughter, Mrs. S McEwan Tomkins, and Miss Marian McEwan. They will spend a month there.- Seattle Times January 27, 1919.

Mr. and Mrs. Alexander Baillie and daughters, Mrs. Samuel Russell and Mrs. Charles H Banks of Connecticut, who've been on an extended trip abroad for several months, will arrive in New York tomorrow, returning home shortly. – Seattle Times June 30 1922.

Mr. Alexander Baillie with his son-in-law, Mr. William Ripley of Tacoma, and his son Alex, is coming home tonight from a fortnights trip to Alaska. – Seattle Times September 4 1922

Mr. and Mrs. Alexander Baillie, who've been at Del Monte for some time, were recently joined by their son-in-law and daughter, commander and Mrs. Isaac C Johnson (Kathleen Baillie). Their other daughters, Mrs. William Ripley of Tacoma, Mrs. Charles Banks of Lakeville Connecticut, and Mrs. Samuel Russell of Seattle, have all been with them for a visit since they went south.- Seattle Times April 3 1924.

Mr. and Mrs. Alexander Baillie, who've been visiting in England and Scotland for several months, will sail for home on the Majestic November 19. – Seattle Times November 7, 1924

Mr. and Mrs. Alexander Baillie of Waloma on American Lake left Tuesday for a fortnight in Yellowstone and Glacier National Parks. Mr. and Mrs. Baillie returned early this spring from a six-month stay in Europe, spent for the most part in Germany, Austria and on the Adriatic. – Seattle Times July 9 1933.

Mr. and Mrs. Alexander Baillie are again at Waloma, their American Lake home, after two months spent at Del Monte and in San Francisco.- Seattle Times April 14, 1935.

Latest word from Mr. and Mrs. Alexander Baillie of Tacoma, who sailed for Europe in September, has been received from Merano, in northern Italy, where they are sojourning after a six week stay in Paris. Mr. and Mrs. Baillie wrote they expected to be in Rome for Christmas. – Seattle Times December 11 1936.

After a winter at Palm Springs, Mr. and Mrs. Alexander Baillie are again established at Waloma, on American Lake. Mrs. William R Ripley, daughter of Mr. Baillie, who spent five months in California this year is also at home, and has taken a cottage at the country club.- Seattle Times May 7, 1939

Alex's travels up and down the West Coast often included stops at the Benbow Inn in Northern California, The Del Monte Hotel in Monterey California, Casa De Manana in La Jolla, and The Hotel Del Coronado in San Diego.

The Brooklyn daily Eagle, New York, for Tuesday, September 20, 1932, gives the ship sailings for that day out of New York. The only ship sailing that day was the United States liner Leviathan. The paper noted that passengers on the Leviathan were Sir William Mitchell, Vice Chancellor of the University of Adelaide Australia, George W Davidson president of the Central Hanover Trust Company, and Alexander Baillie president of the Rainier National Park Company.

In 1948 Alex was in La Jolla staying at the Casa De Manana. While there he met Izetta Jewel (Stage actress, woman's rights activist, politician, and radio personality) who asked him to do a radio interview (Interview is on You Tube under Alexander Baillie, golf). Alex did the interview where he was asked to describe briefly the history of golf. At the end of the interview he was then asked to sing a favorite Scottish song "A Wee Deoch an Doris" which Izetta had heard him sing the night before at the hotel. The words to the song are as follows:

Wee Deoch an Doris

There's a good old Scottish custom that has stood the test o'time,
It's a custom that's been carried out in every land and clime.
When brother Scots are gathered, it's aye the usual thing,
Just before we say good night, we fill our cups and sing...

Chorus
Just a wee deoch an doris, just a wee drop, that's all.
Just a wee deoch an doris afore ye gang awa.
There's a wee wifie waitin' in a wee but an ben.
If you can say, "It's a braw bricht moonlicht nicht",
Then yer a'richt, ye ken.

Now I like a man that is a man; a man that's straight and fair.
The kind of man that will and can, in all things do his share.
Och, I like a man a jolly man, the kind of man, you know,
The chap that slaps your back and says, "Jock, just before ye go..."

Chorus

Meaning of unusual words:
deoch an doris=Gaelic for a drink at the door, a last farewell drink
aye=always
but and ben=a two-roomed cottage
ken=know

*****

On Friday October 22, 1948, a dinner was held at the Tacoma Country Club in honor of Alex recognizing his contribution to golf in the Northwest. Some 150 friends from Washington, Oregon, and British Columbia were in attendance. The following three images are from the program given to all the guests.

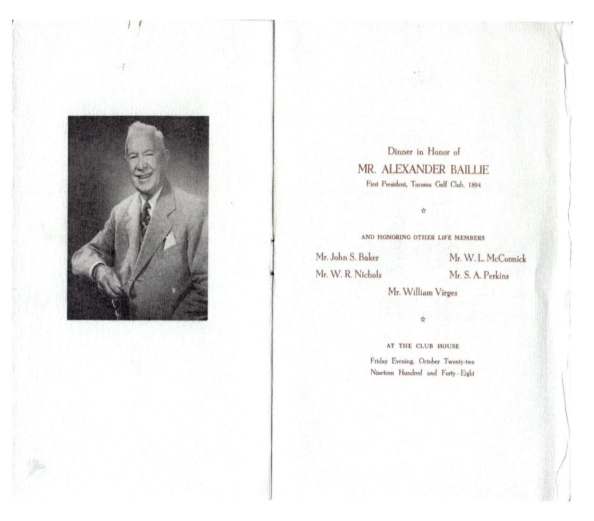

MENU

☆

Fresh Crablegs on Hearts of Artichokes
and sliced Avocado

☆

Consommé Royal   Duff Gordon Sherry
"Nina"

☆

Roast Prime Ribs of Beef au Jus

Yorkshire Pudding   Beaulieu Signature
Burgundy 1944
Roast Potatoes

String Beans, Bavarian Style

☆

Frozen Egg Nog with Macaroons   Gotham Brut
Champagne

☆

Nuts   Mints

Café

PROGRAM

☆

MR. RENO ODLIN
Toastmaster

☆

Dinner Music

Miss Kathryn Porter   Mr. Walton McKinney
Soprano   Tenor

Mr. Mel Hansen
Pianist

☆

Male Quartette
The Mountaineers

☆

The Toast "To the Life Members"
MR. FRANK S. BAKER

☆

The Toast to "ALEX"
MR. WILLIAM P. CAMERON
SEATTLE

☆

Response
MR. ALEXANDER BAILLIE

Presentation
MR. AUDSLEY FRASER

GENERAL COMMITTEE

Mr. J. W. Reynolds, Chm.   Mr. G. E. Karlen   Mr. Roscoe A. Smith
Mr. Byron D. Scott   Mr. Warren Y. Hull   Mr. Will Maylon
                           Mr. Larry Huseby

☆

INVITATION COMMITTEE

Mr. G. Corydon Wagner, Jr., Chm.   Mr. L. T. Murray
Mr. Charles H. Ingram   Mr. C. D. Hunter, Jr.
Mr. Everett Griggs   Mr. J. P. Weyerhaeuser, Jr.

☆

DECORATIONS

Mrs. Charles Pasco, Chm.   Mrs. Cyrus Happy   Mrs. A. W. Clapp
Ms. Corydon Wagner, Jr.   Mrs. Audsley Fraser   Mrs. Hilding Lindberg
Mrs. Thomas Murray   Mrs. Wayne Keyes   Mrs. Elizabeth Fogg
                           Mrs. G. E. Karlen

☆

Should auld acquaintance be forgot,
And never brought to mind?
Should auld acquaintance be forgot,
And days of auld lang syne?

Alex on left all decked out in his kilt for the big dinner. His good friend Audsley Fraser is on the right. (Tacoma Public Library image)

Guests at party honoring Alex. Alex is at center rear, short person with white hair. (Tacoma Public Library image)

Alex with picture of himself as a young golfer (Tacoma Public Library image)

Alex was again back at Casa De Manana in February of 1949 and while there he wrote the following letter to his grandson Alexander Ripley, who went by Alec. (Family always called Alex "Gramp".)

Sunday 6 February 1949

casa de mañana
the house of 'TOMORROW'
LA JOLLA California

My dear Alec,

Affectionate greetings to you, the sweet darling Mary and the two young Tycoons from "Mud" & me and to thank you for the 25 iron men for St Dunstans and in lieu thereof I am sending to Lady Fraser 2-10 + 1-5 dollar bills. I usually buy a Draft on London and at $4.05 Exchange get £6.3.9. but as St. Dunstans buy a lot of things in the U.S. they can always use dollars to advantage and Lady Forres can hand these bills to the management of St Dunstans & get sterling for them & I gave her a tip about the exchange. All is well with "mum" and me - weather is improving & today is perfect. Well two weeks from yesterday we will greet you here with open arms, feed and shelter you all

casa de mañana
the house of 'TOMORROW'
LA JOLLA California

and unless you & Mary have joined the teetotal brigade we will be able to supply you with alcoholic beverages in moderation, if only for the purpose of keeping your elbows supple.

Much love

Gramp.

One family possession which Alex treasured was a grandfather clock. About 6 weeks after I was born he sent me a letter (which I still have) describing the history of the clock. Alex describes it as an 8-day clock made in Brechin by James Christie in September of 1792 and sold to Alexander Baillie for ten shillings. It then passed to his son Alexander Baillie in July of 1815, one month after the battle of Waterloo. It came into the possession of Alex's father in 1840 and remained with them until his mother died in 1905. One of Alex's sisters took care of it until 1908, when it was then crated and sent by rail from Brechin to Glasgow, where it was loaded on the sailing ship "City of Benares". It came around Cape Horn and arrived in Tacoma after a voyage of 145 days. The crate had been packed in dried onions in order to prevent worms. The clock passed to Alexander Baillie Ripley a few years before Alex's death and currently sits in my living room.

Clock face showing the manufacture's name and Brechin. The four corners of the face are depictions of the four elements earth, air, water, and fire.

Clock is made of Mahogany

Alex had a great sense of humor, which had a lot to do with why so many enjoyed his company. Alex always enjoyed reading the comics in the newspaper, and it was not unusual to see him relaxing as in the picture below.

Alex was a man of the highest character, and his integrity won him a wide reputation in the world of business. His genial nature and his sturdy Scottish characteristics gained him the affection of many. He numbered among his friends men and women from all over the world. Mary Ripley, wife of Alex's grandson, remembers Alex as a real "people person" who loved telling stories. She remembers "his keen wit and mind" and how kind he was to her as a newlywed to his grandson.

Alex loved the outdoors and one of his passions other than golf was fly fishing.

Mrs. William R Ripley is the guest of her mother Mrs. Alexander Baillie while her husband is away on a fishing trip. The fishing party is composed of Mr. Alexander Baillie, Mr. F T Crowe, Mr. George B Nicoll

(Mrs. Alexander Baillie's brother), Mr. William R Ripley and son Master Alexander Ripley, of Tacoma, and Master Jack Crowe. They expect to return after Labor Day. Seattle Times August 30, 1919.

The small son (he was 11) *of Mr. and Mrs. William Ripley, of Tacoma, Alex, is going north with his grandfather, Mr. Alexander Baillie, who will sail July 2 on the Spokane for Alaska for a several weeks fishing trip. Mr. Walter McEwan Tompkins and Mr. George Nicoll also are going with Mr. Baillie* – Seattle Times June 24, 1921

1940 fishing trip to Park Lake B.C.

He loved taking his grandsons, Alexander Ripley and Bill Johnson, out fishing in the Cascades. He always made sure they were up river from him so if they fell in he could grab them as they went by. He would also make trips to Alaska to go fishing. There are a number of ship's registries showing him traveling to Ketchikan to go fishing. Hanging in his house was a painting by William Keith (a well-known Scottish artist who lived much of his life in California) that showed a stream very similar to those that Alex would fish.

William Keith Painting

This is a Sydney Lawrence painting of the Tacoma Balfour Guthrie docks. It was given to Alex's daughter Elizabeth when she was married in 1911. We believe Alex commissioned Sydney Lawrence to create the painting.

Alex was very close to his three grandsons, particularly Alexander Ripley and Bill Johnson. Bill Johnson lived with Alex and Ida during much of his teenage years as Bill's mother Kathleen had serious alcohol issues and his father had gone off with another woman. Alex had actually gone to Los Angeles and brought Bill Johnson home with him because Kathleen could not take proper care of Bill. Alex helped pay for a lot of Bill's education at Hotchkiss, Shawnigan Lake School, and the University of Washington. Bill joined the army where he eventually became a Captain in the Transportation Corp. He then went on to a career in the timber industry in Eugene, Oregon where he owned the Eugene – Willamette Lumber Company. Through his work Bill became good friends with George Weyerhaeuser. Alex was also the best man in Bill's first wedding in June of 1941 when he married Althea Cunningham in Chicago.

RAINIER NATIONAL PARK COMPANY

OFFICERS
ALEXANDER BAILLIE President
S. L. BARNES Vice President
F. R. GRIFFITHS Secretary-Treasurer
P. H. SCEVA General Manager
W. W. FRANKLAND Mgr. of Transportation and Purchasing Depts.

DIRECTORS
ALEXANDER BAILLIE
S. L. BARNES
JOHN DOWER
JOHN W. EDDY
A. M. FRASER
RAYMOND R. FRAZIER
EVERETT G. GRIGGS II
S. H. HEDGES
A. H. LANDRAM
F. D. METZGER
S. M. MORRIS
L. T. MURRAY
H. A. RHODES
VOLNEY RICHMOND, Jr.
W. V. TANNER
WILLIAM VIRGES
DAVID WHITCOMB
HERBERT WITHERSPOON

GENERAL OFFICE
TACOMA, WASHINGTON

November 6, 1940

William B. Johnson, Esquire
Wheeler Osgood Sales Corporation
122 South Michigan Avenue
Chicago, Illinois

My dear Bill:

   Many thanks for your letter of 2nd instant with all your news and Aunt Ida and I were interested to have you tell us that you had been appointed by the Board of Election Commissioners to watch out for crooked voting yesterday. Well, the battle has been fought and won by Mr. Roosevelt by a very substantial majority. Aunt Ida and I voted for Wilkie and we were disappointed that he was not the choice of the people but Mr. Roosevelt's election proves that he has a majority of the voters satisfied that he is the right man to lead the country for another four years.

   There was a lot of mud slinging during the campaign and if anyone deplores this, I do, but it has been ever thus and so we must take things as they go in a Democracy. We have many problems to solve in this country but I have faith in the American people and in their leaders and now that Mr. Roosevelt will continue to have his seat in the White House, I am one hundred percent for him. But I do hope he will make some changes in his cabinet and I think he will.

   And now to rather a painful subject in connection with two of my grandsons, Alexander B. Ripley of Los Angeles, and William B. Johnson, of Chicago. According to facts, each of them owe me five iron men and I have just written to Mr. Ripley that a remittance will be welcomed, at his convenience. I thought of sending you a wire and Alex also, but that would have cost me a dollar and a half and I don't want to have the total amount of $10.00 impaired in any way as I propose investing this money and earmarking it to use when I am an old man.

page 2

>   We plan to get away to Palm Springs about the end of next
> week and Aunt Ida has started to pack already.
>
>   I note business continues good and now that the election
> is over and that feature of the country's life settled, I feel that
> industry will go steadily forward and that the Wheeler Osgood Company
> will have all the business it can take for the next two or three years.
> The taxes, of course, are going to make a terrible crimp in our profits
> but this is something we can't help. As regards the bonuses, Mr. Babbitt
> and Mr. Fischer, at the Bank of California, and myself are on a committee
> to make a recommendation to the Board as to what these bonuses should be
> and we will have a meeting in the next few days to deal with the subject.
>
>   In the meantime, love from Aunt Ida and me and assuring
> you that it gives me great pleasure to think I made a safe bet,
>
>   Yours affectionately,
>   ALEXANDER BAILLIE

This is a letter that Alex sent Bill Johnson in 1940. There was clearly a bet that Bill and Alec had lost to Alex and Alex was making a "tongue in cheek" reminder that they each owed him $5.00.

Alex also paid the tuition for Alec Ripley to go to the Shawnigan Lake School on Vancouver Island from 1923 to 1927. While Alec was in school there, the main building was destroyed by fire. At the time Alec was a prefect and "Head of School". To help with the rebuilding, Alex made a contribution in his grandson's name. We assume the contribution was significant as one of the Houses (dorms) is still named Ripley House.

Alex with his three grandsons Alec Ripley (with son William), Montgomery Russell, and Bill Johnson.

*****

In September 1949 Alex was nearing his 90th birthday. Alex anticipated celebrating his 90th birthday on Friday the 9th at a luncheon in Seattle at the Rainier Club. Then a few family and friends were to come to Waloma for dinner that night. But on Wednesday September 7, 1949, two days before his 90th birthday, Alex was out in the rose garden shortly before noon at his Waloma home in Tacoma picking flowers for a friend, Mr. William Virgis, who like Alex was just 90. Alex collapsed and died of a heart attack while performing this act of friendship so typical of him. He had previously been in good health and had maintained his keen wit and mind right up to the time of his death. Services were held at Alex's Waloma home. Alex is buried in the Tacoma Cemetery near his wife Jessie and his daughters Kathleen and Marian.

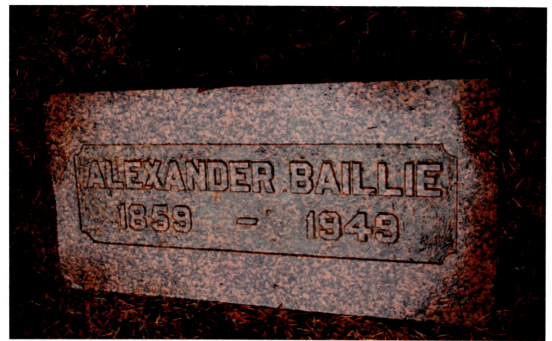
Alex's gravestone at the Tacoma Cemetery

An article in the Seattle Times shortly after his death described Alex as "one of Scotland's gifts to the world, a ray of sunshine and a beneficent and constructive force in the Pacific Northwest. In him were all of the best qualities of the Scottish character-sterling integrity, devotion to the public wheel, loyalty to the highest ideals in every attitude of life, a rare gift of friendship, a personality that radiated good cheer and a delightful sense of humor". A few days before his death he wrote an old friend from Paradise Inn on Mount Rainier the following: "Good morning at 8:10 AM dear old friend. A heavenly day it is as I look out on the majestic Mount Rainier I say out loud, "great are thy works oh God." He had recently said with a smile "whenever the call comes I am ready, and I have no fear."

An estate sale was held in 1950 at Waloma. An ad in the Seattle Times stated the following:

Furnishings from the estate of the late Mrs. Alexander Baillie including antique Italian furniture, 90th Chickering parlor grand piano, carved dining room set in red damask, lovely China, Venetian glass, beautiful furniture and bric-a-brac.- Seattle Times, January 25, 1950.

Timeline:

1859 –
Alexander Baillie born

1874 –
Alex graduates from high school and starts working at the Royal Bank of Scotland in Brechin

1879 –
Alex moves to Liverpool and starts working for Balfour Williams & Company

1880 –
Alex transferred to Portland

1885 –
Alex marries Jessie Nicoll

1888 –
Alex transferred to Tacoma

1894 –
Alexander Baillie started the Tacoma Country Club

1898 –
Alexander Baillie became a US citizen

1904 –
Acquired property for current location of Tacoma Country Club

1907 –
Alexander Baillie made partner in Balfour Guthrie Company

1914 –
Alexander Baillie moved to Seattle

1926 –
Alex's wife Jessie dies

1928 –
Alex marries Ida

1929 –
Alex moved back to Tacoma
Alex made president of Rainier National Park Company

1930 –
Alexander Baillie made President of Balfour Guthrie Corporation

1931 –
Alex retires from Balfour Guthrie Company

1944 –
Alex's wife Ida dies
Alex made Chairman of the Board of Rainier National Park Company

1949 –
Alexander Baillie died on September 7th

References:

"Fore! Golf lands in Gearhart"- McMenamins

Tacoma News Tribune

Seattle Times

"Wonderland: An Administrative History of Mount Rainier National Park" – Theodore Catton

"The Tacoma Country and Golf Club 1894-1994" – Shirlee H. Smith

"Balfour Guthrie & Company Limited, A First Century of Commerce 1869 – 1969" Balfour Guthrie & Company

Made in the USA
Las Vegas, NV
21 August 2022